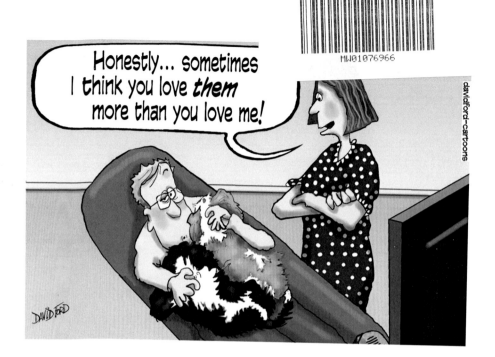

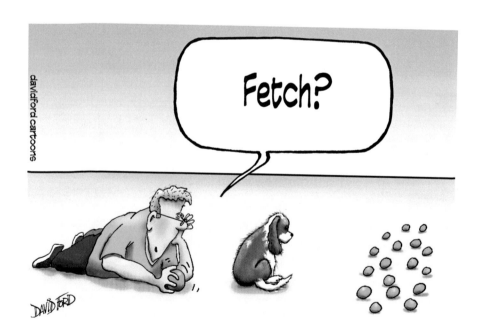

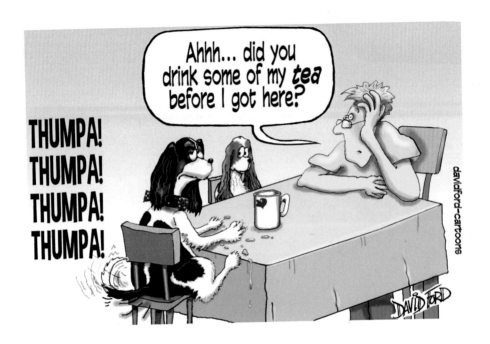

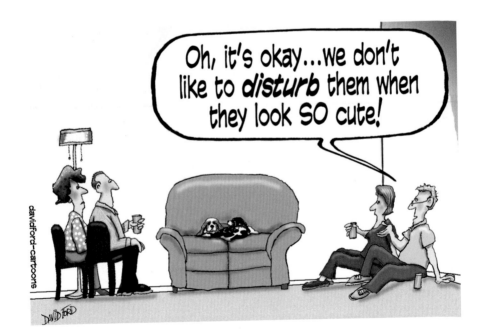

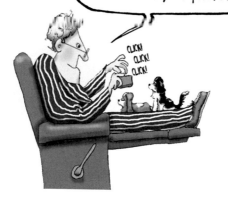

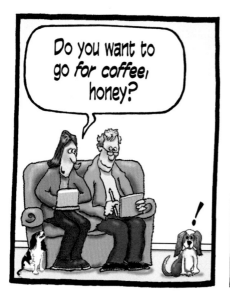

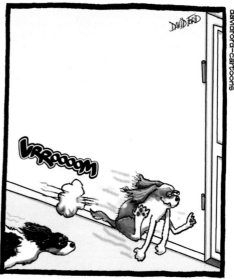

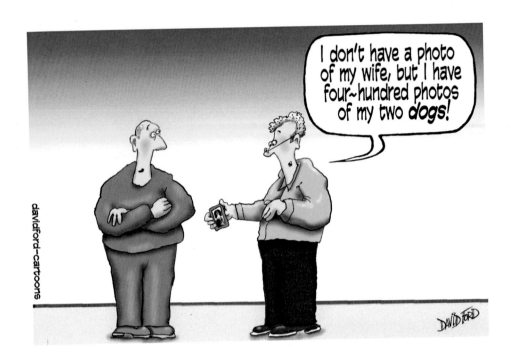

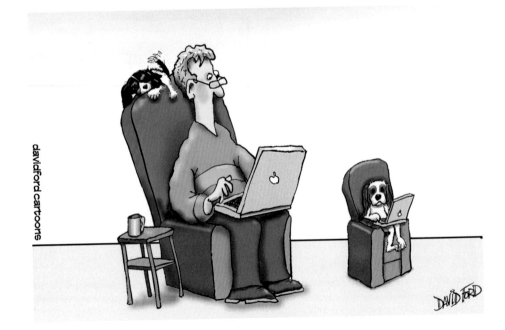

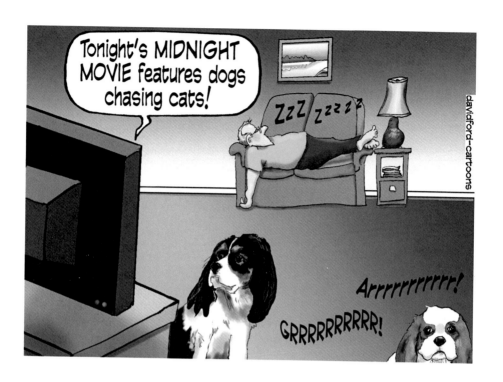
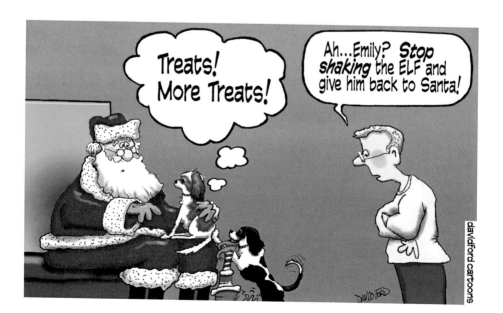

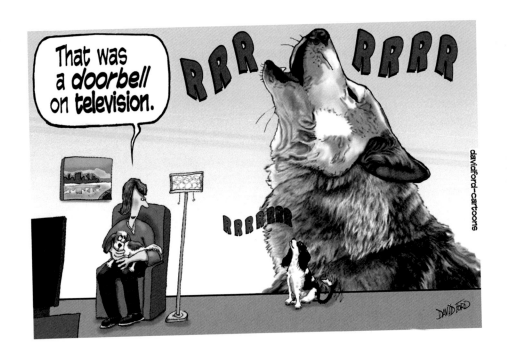

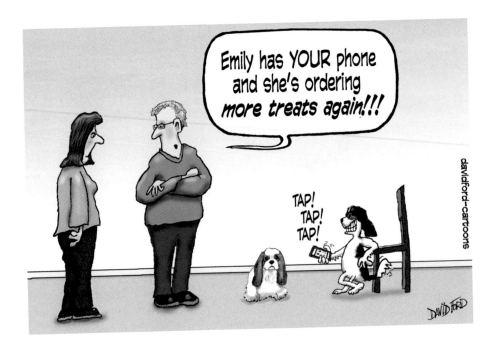

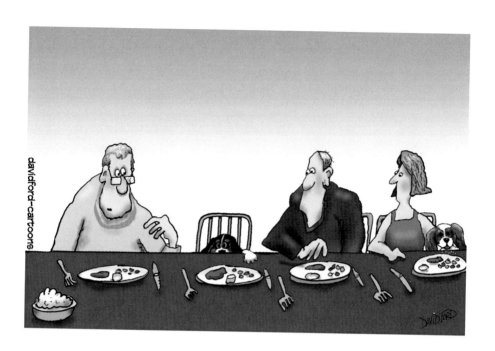

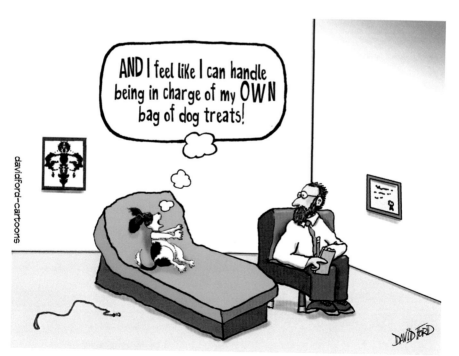

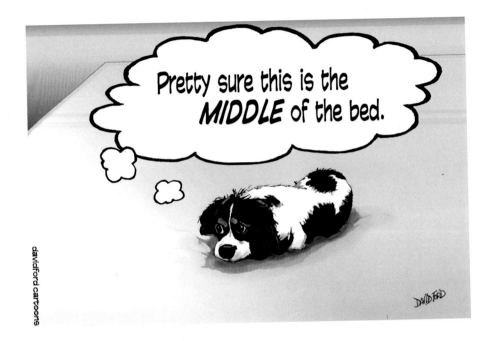

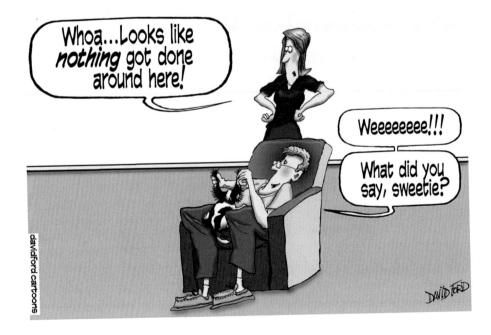

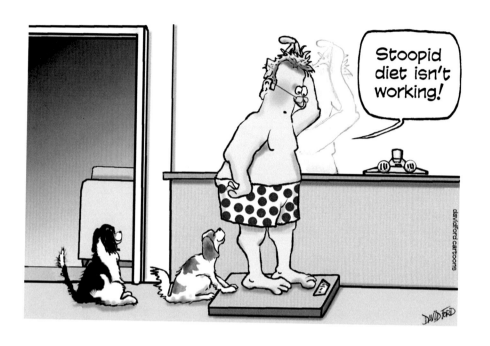

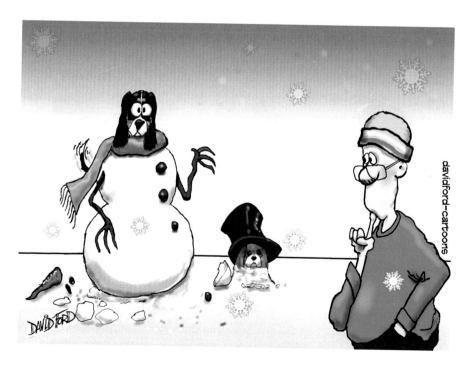

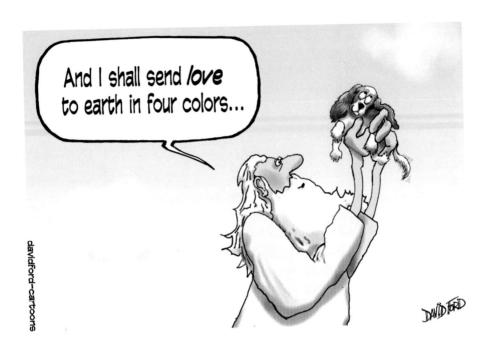

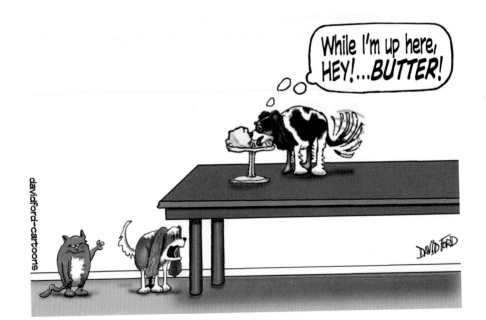

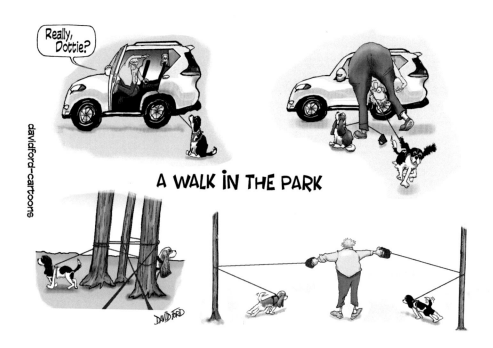

A WALK IN THE PARK

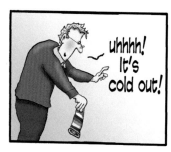

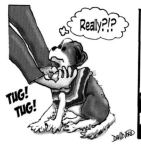

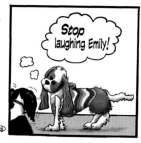

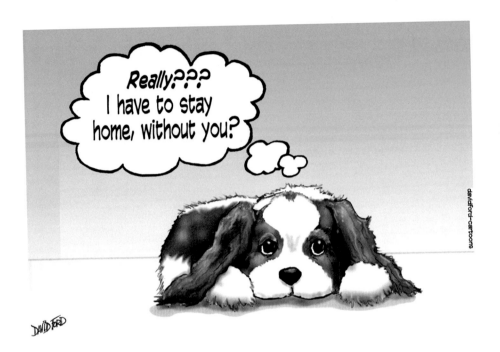

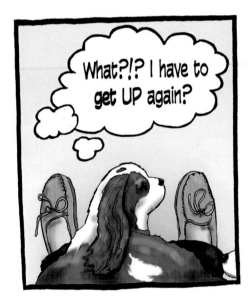

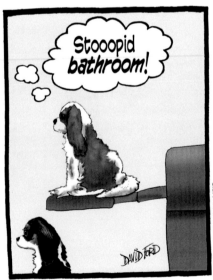

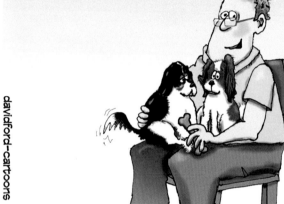

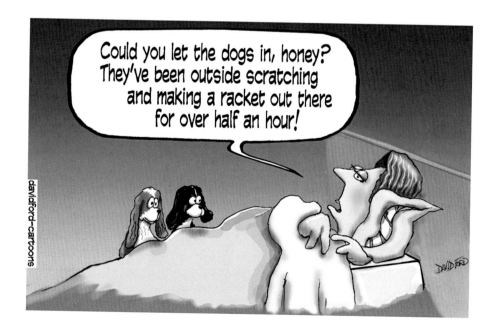

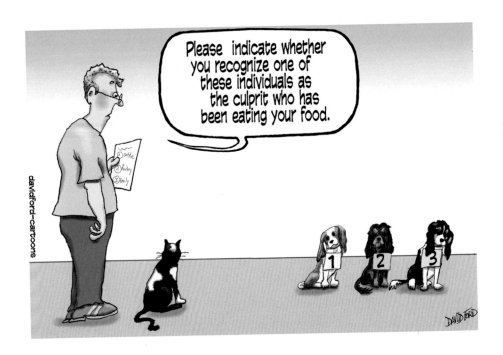

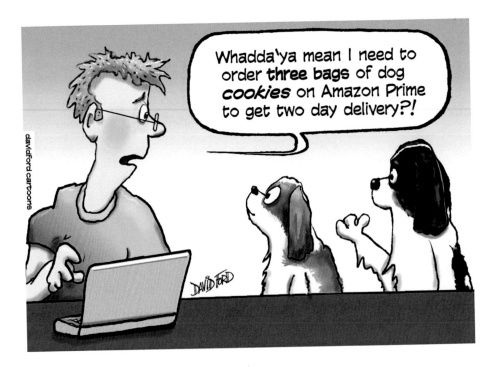

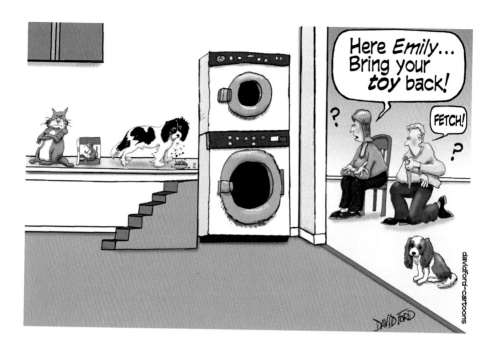

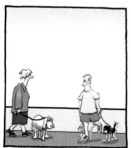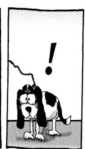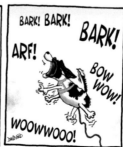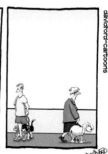

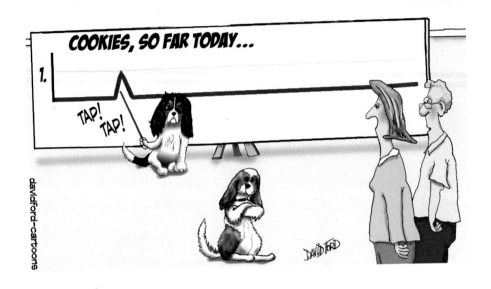

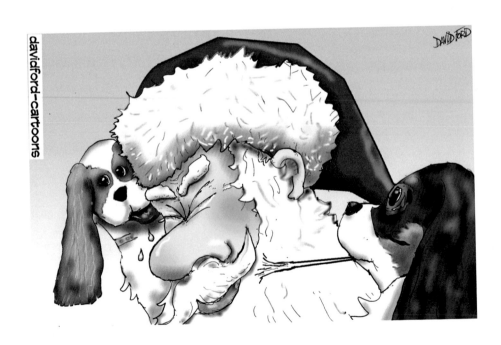

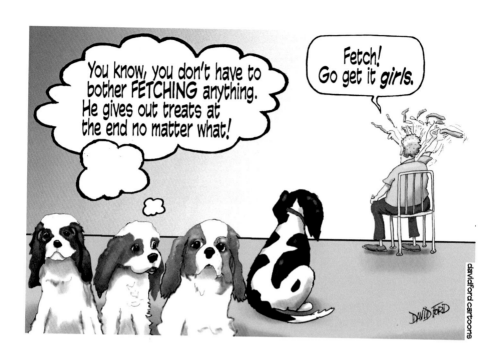

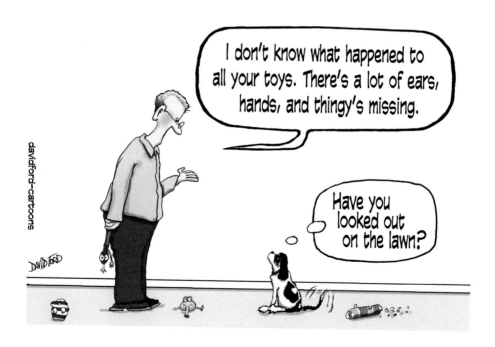

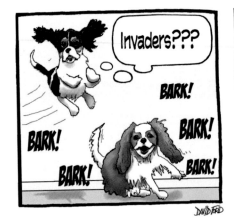
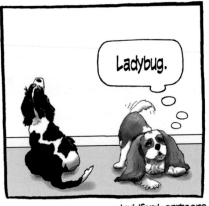

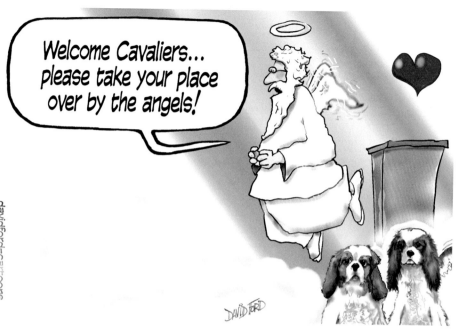

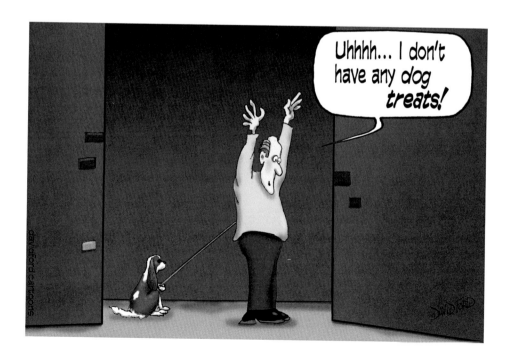

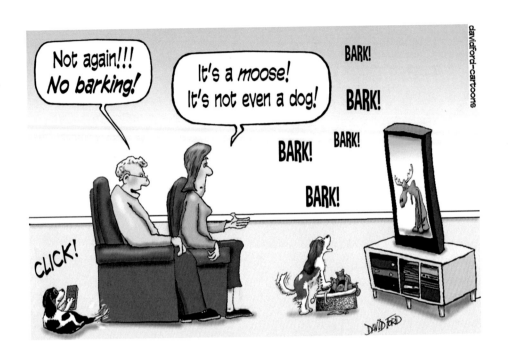
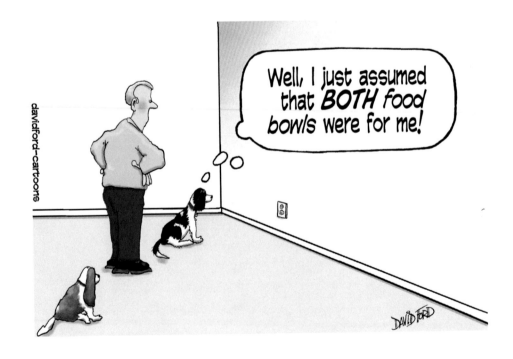

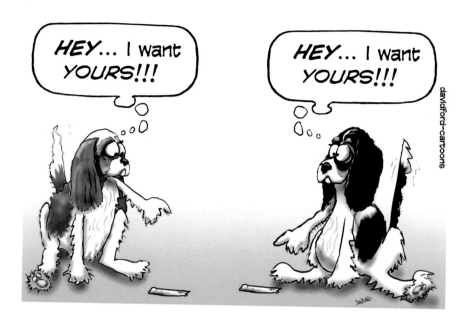

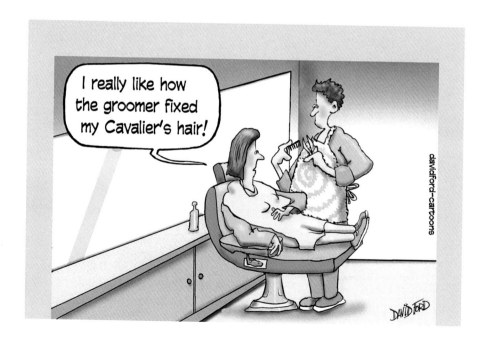

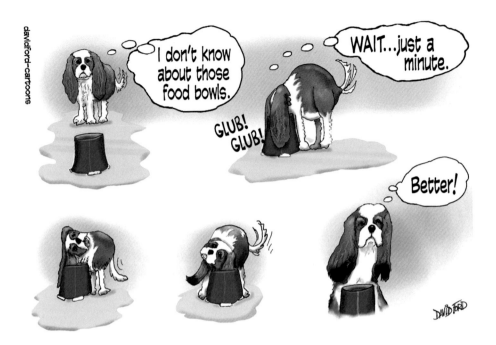

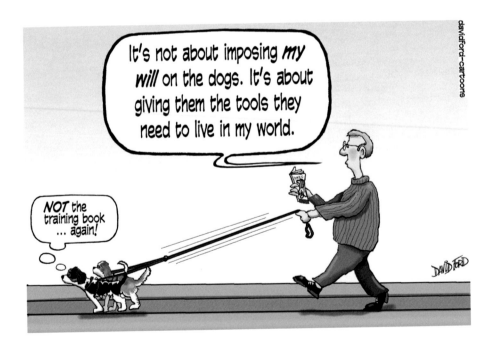

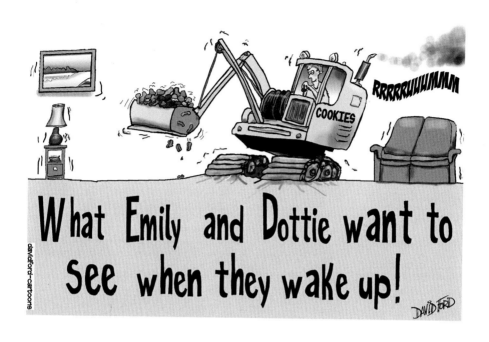

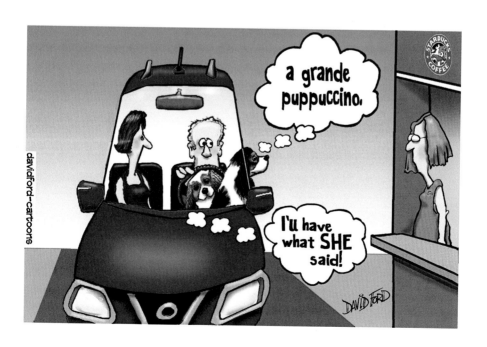

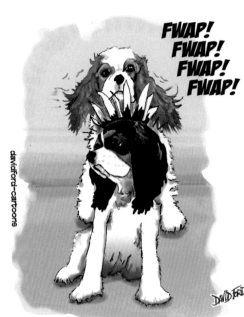

FWAP!
FWAP!
FWAP!
FWAP!

EMILY IS OUR
    TAIL~WAGGER,

DOTTIE IS OUR
    TAIL~WAGEE!

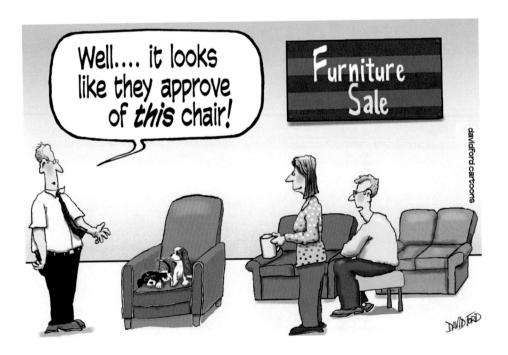

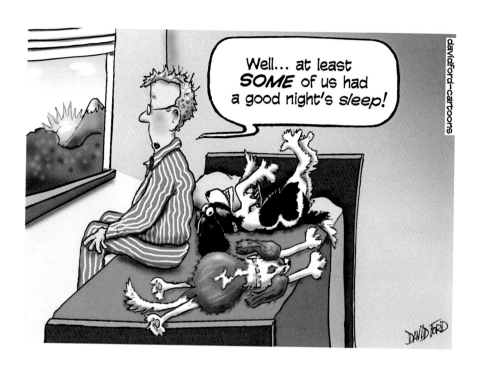

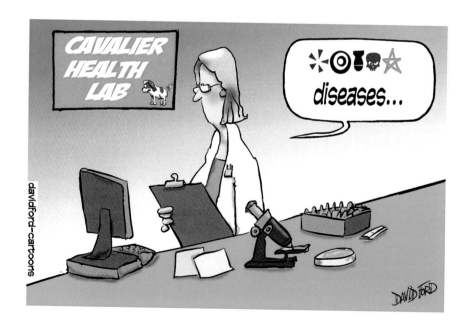

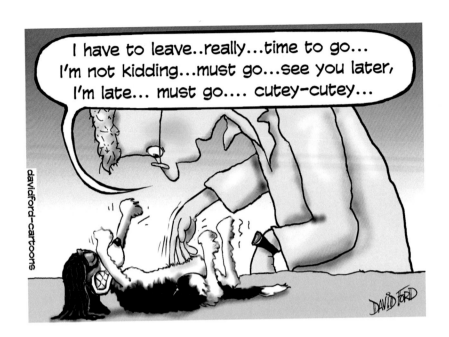

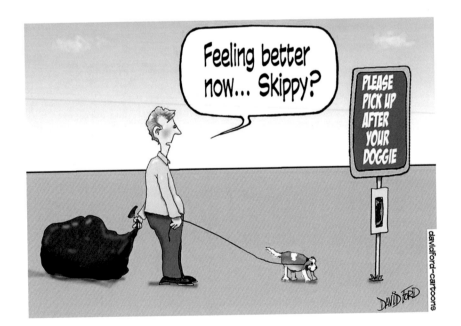

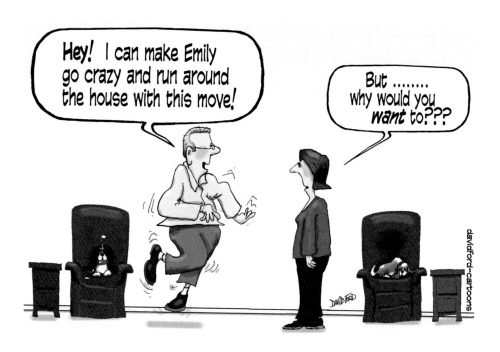

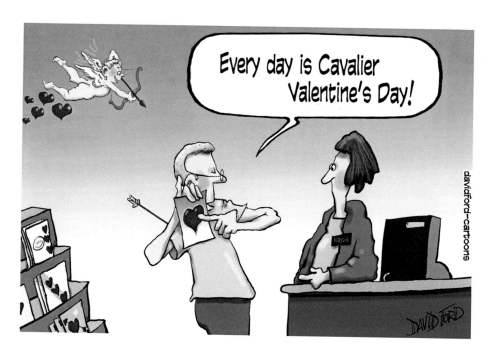

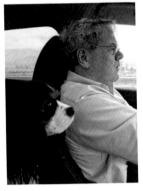

Our sweet girls, Dottie and Emily.

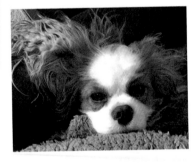

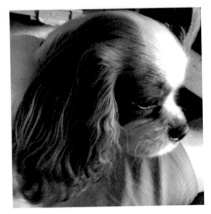

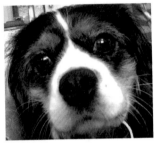

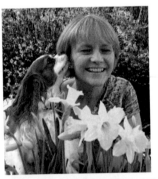

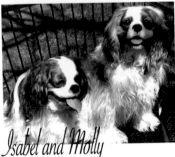

Isabel and Molly

13016578R00019

Made in the USA
Lexington, KY
29 October 2018